High Desert Walk

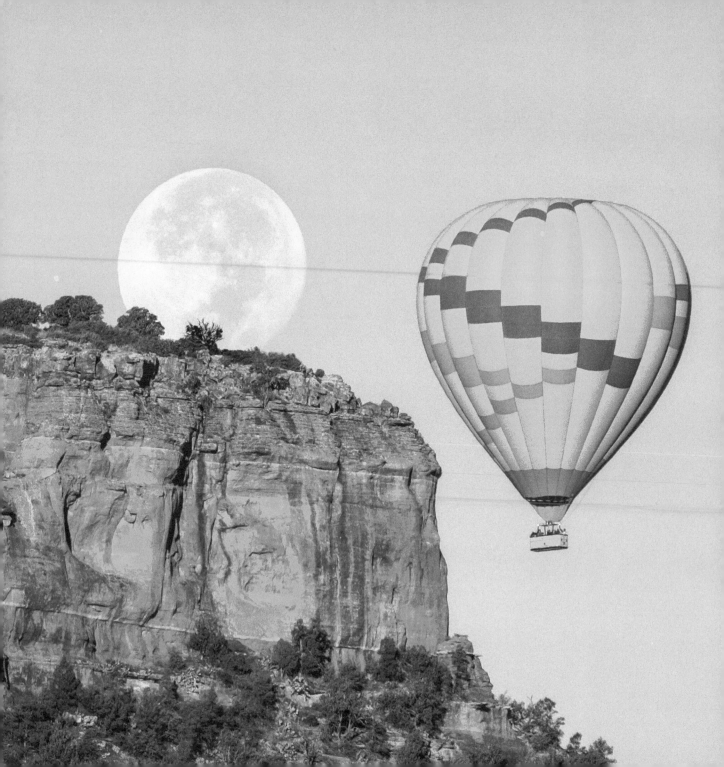

High Desert Walk

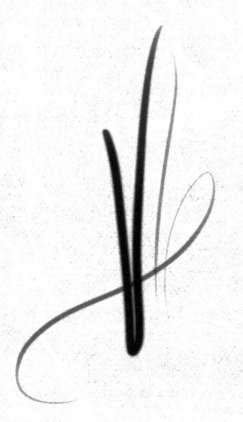

 Blair Mathews | HAIKU

 Kimmy Tran | ZEN INK

 David Martin | PHOTOGRAPHS

Airen Press
MADISON, WISCONSIN

WITH THANKS TO

KIMMY TRAN | Calligrapher
Whose Zen Ink Renderings Give the Haiku Voice

DAVID MARTIN | Photographer, Sedona
For his Creative Energy

ANNA STEVENSON | Editor, Madison
She with keen vision

KAREN BICKERS | Alpha Graphics, Madison
For her Steady Advice and Support

KAREN JOHNSON MATHEWS | For Being

 Airen Press
1240 Wellesley Road | Madison, Wi 53705
bmathews@wisc.edu

CONTENTS

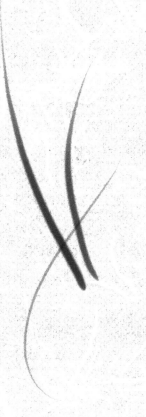

Whisper

Meaning's Voice,
Clearer than
Spoken Word,
Listen.

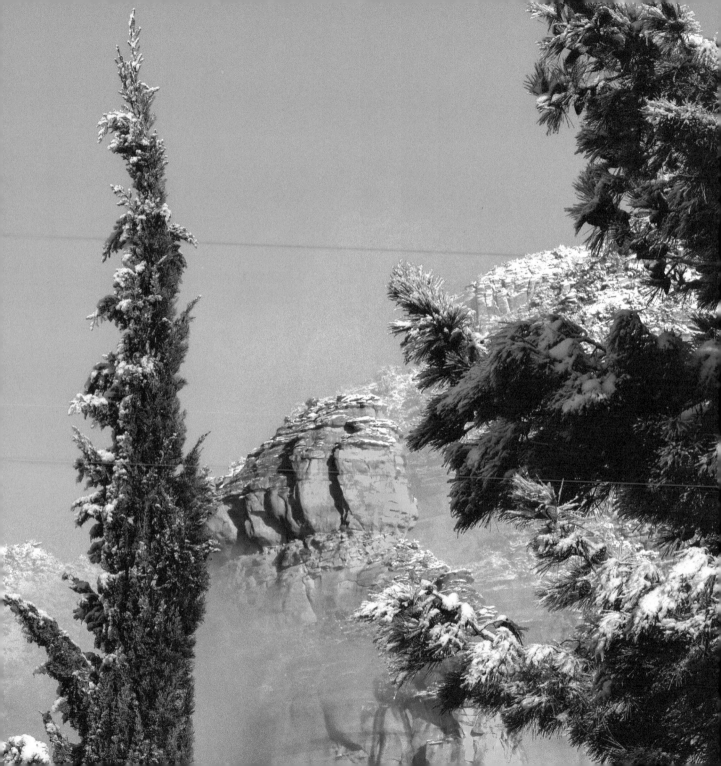

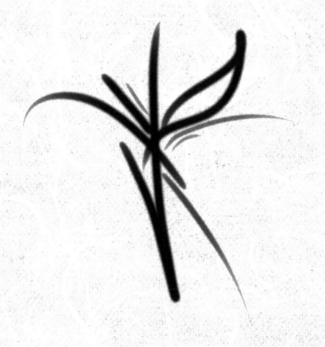

Peek

Beauty in shyness,
Cautious smile,
Constrained promise,
Invitation to self,
Others.

3

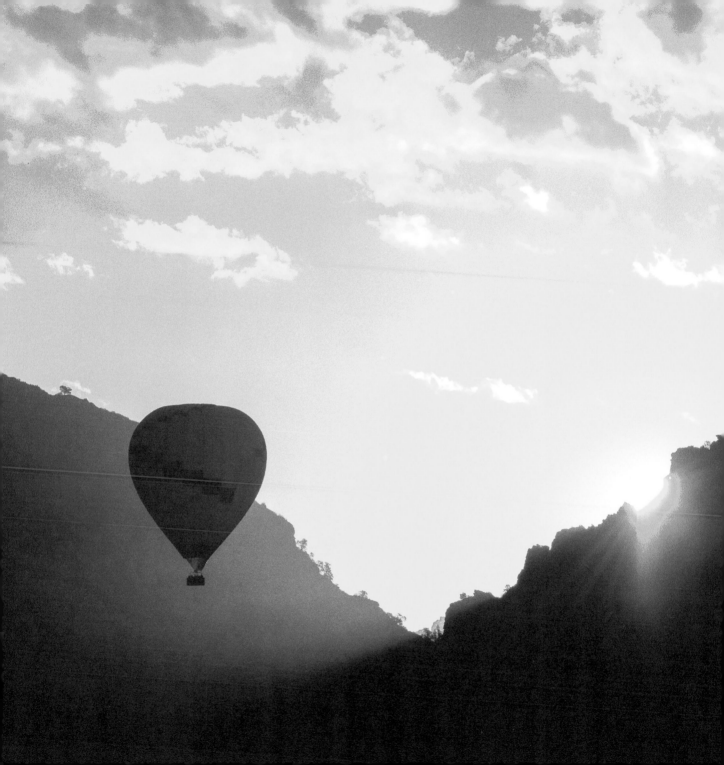

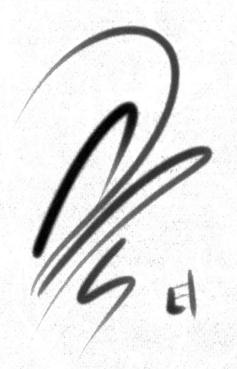

Night Dancer

Grayish white cosmic
Energy waves
Dance outside window,
Heart mind's pillow.

5

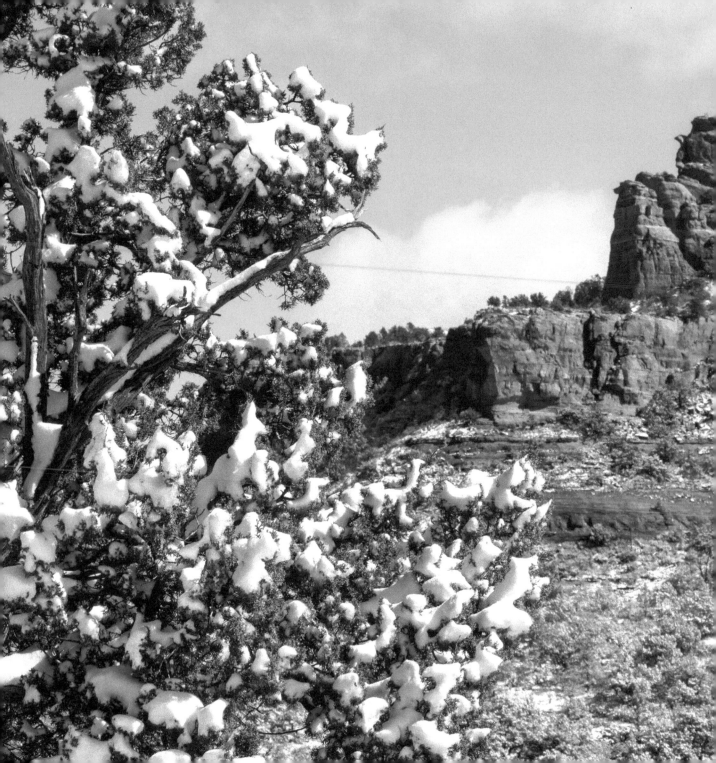

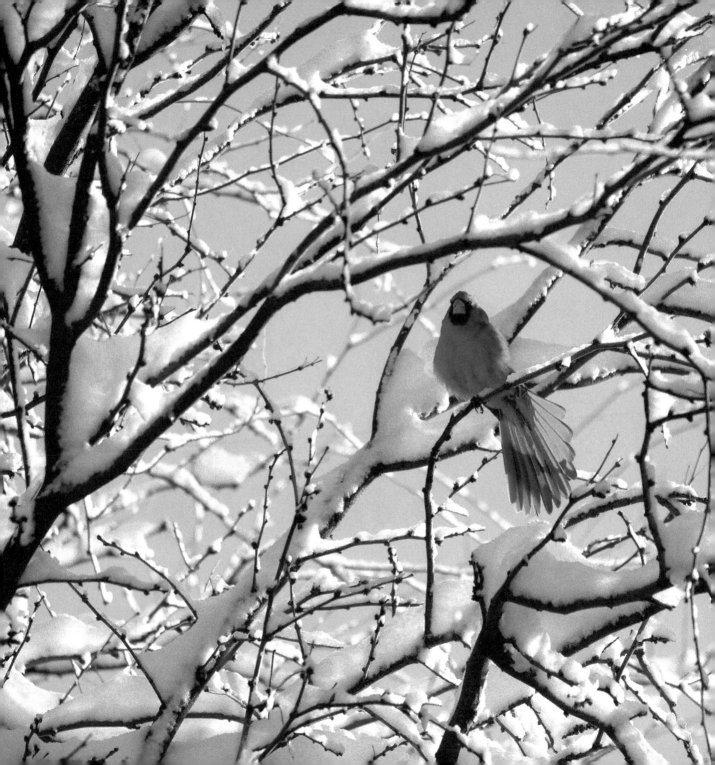

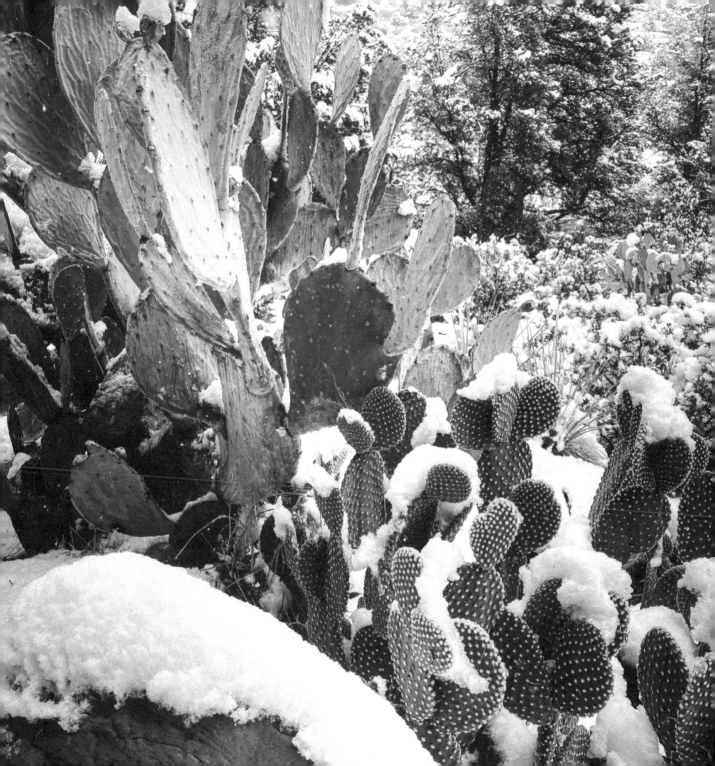

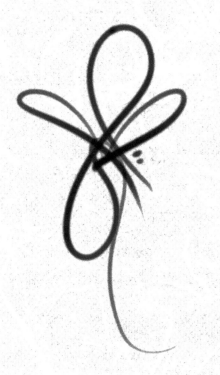

Physician

Respect,
Love,
Secured,
Knot by
Knot.

9

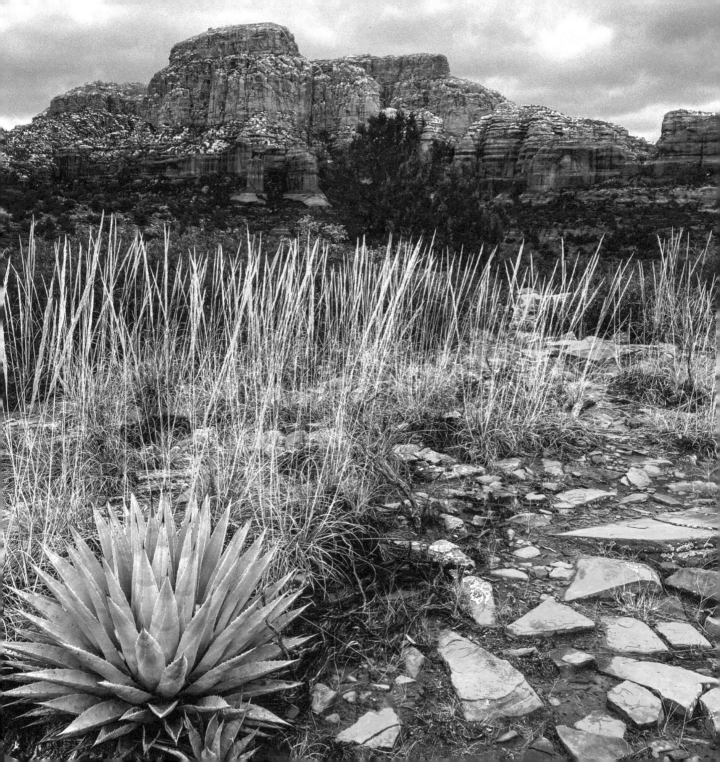

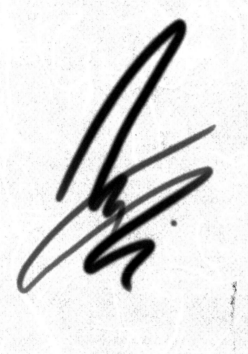

Vortex

Good friend passes,
Great Grand Daughter born,
Same time, Same place,
Life's vortex.

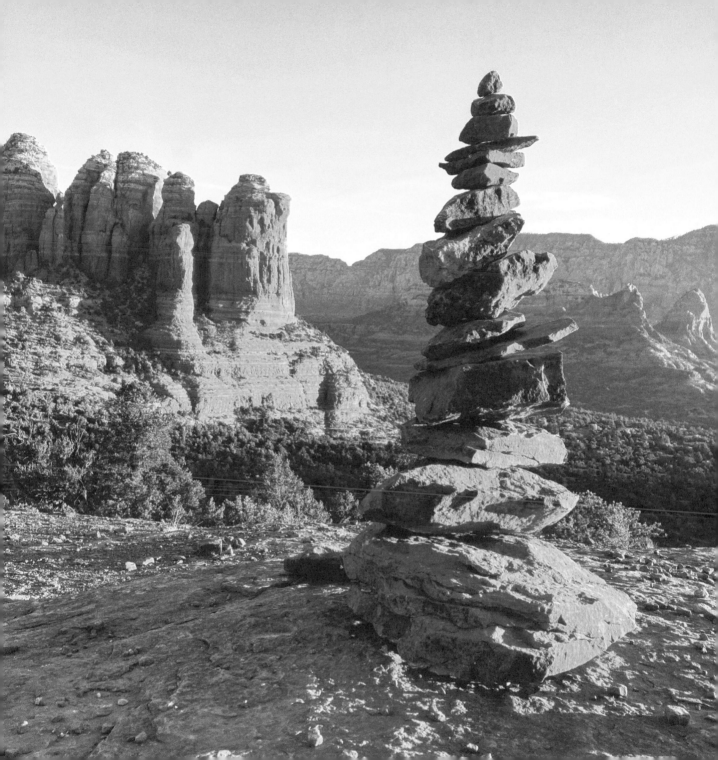

Rest

Deep grief,
love's measure,
Together,
At last.

13

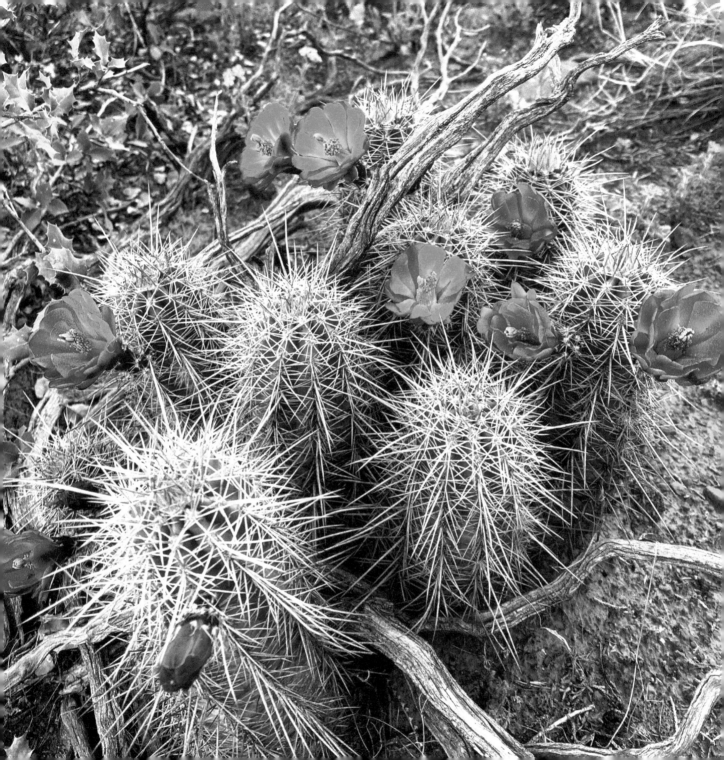

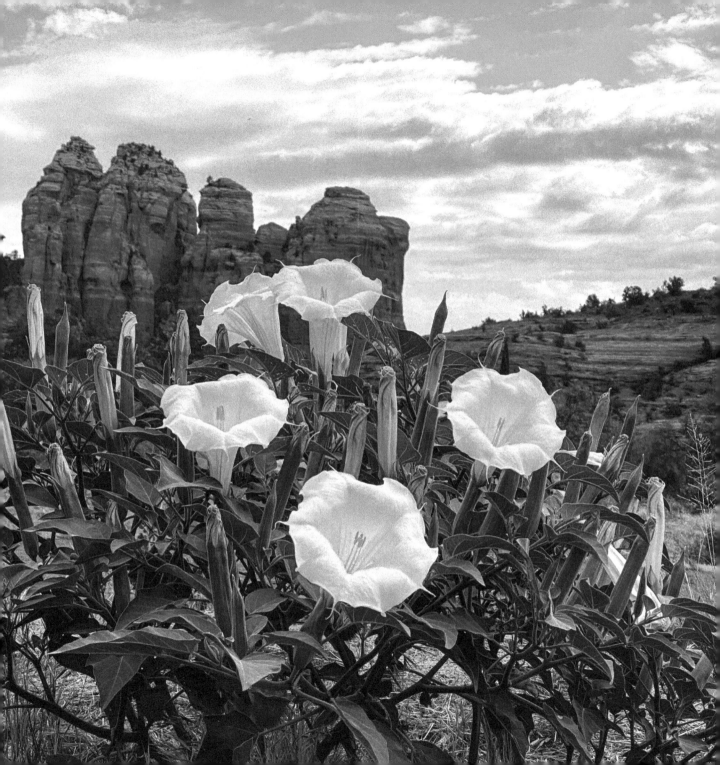

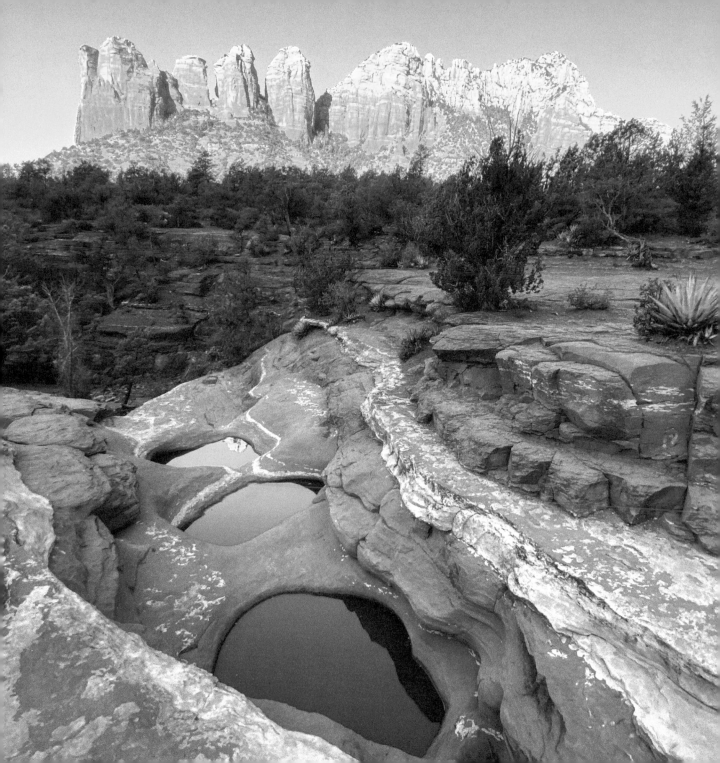

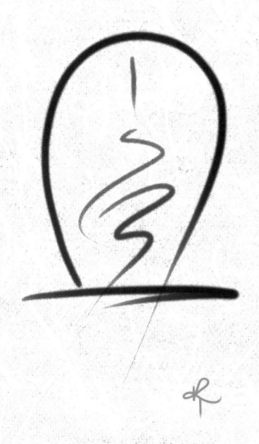

Transition

Sitting still,
Preparing path,
This world,
Other world.

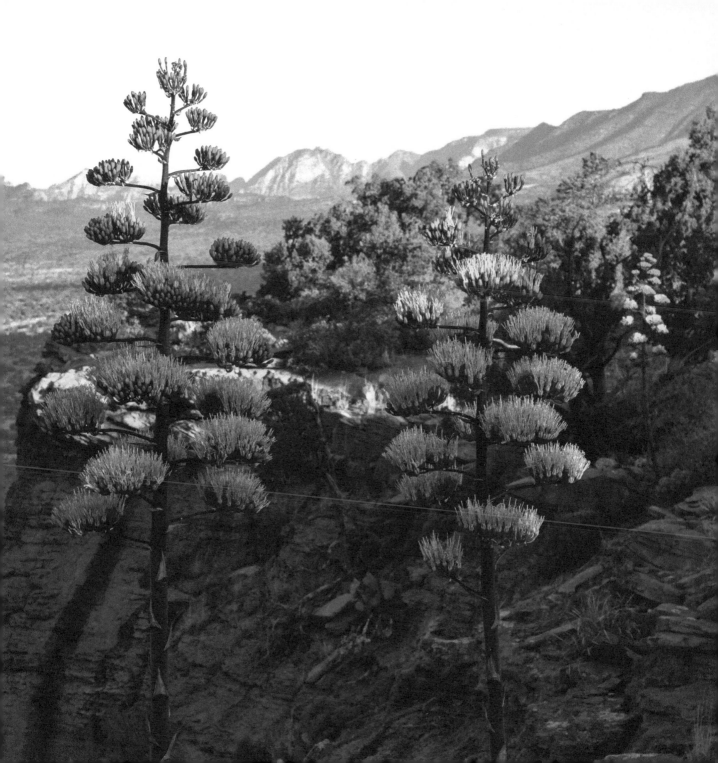

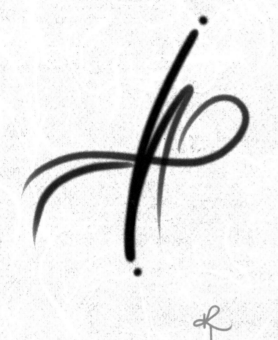

Foreshortened

Quiet fellow,
Passing by,
Passing on,
Before his time.

19

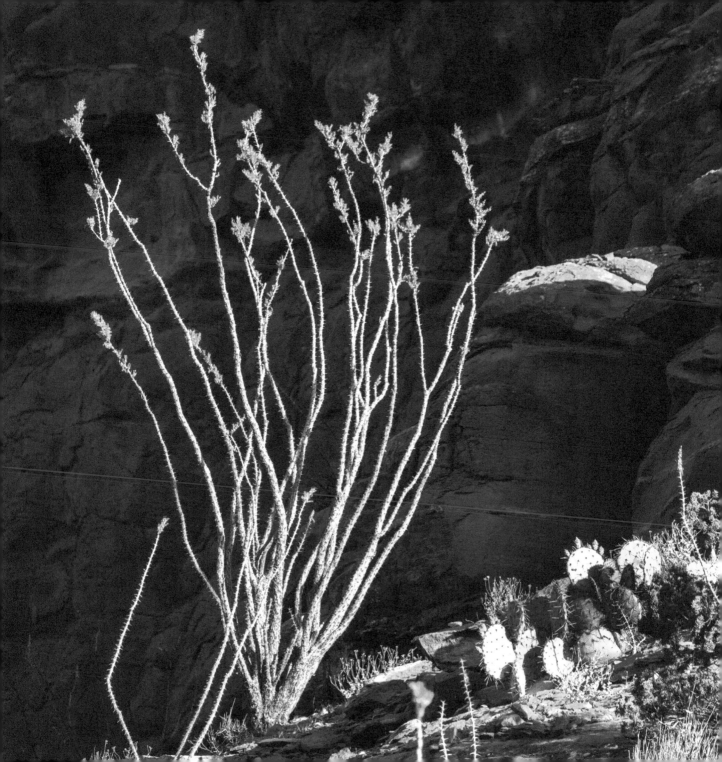

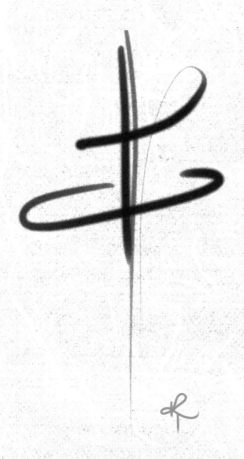

Enter

Breath in,
Enter quiet,
Place within,
Breath out,
Reside within.

21

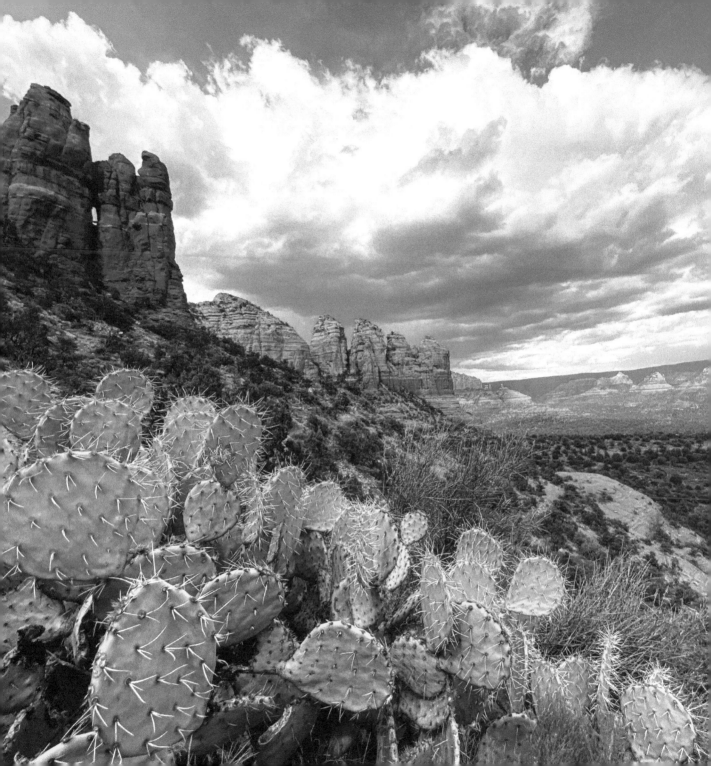

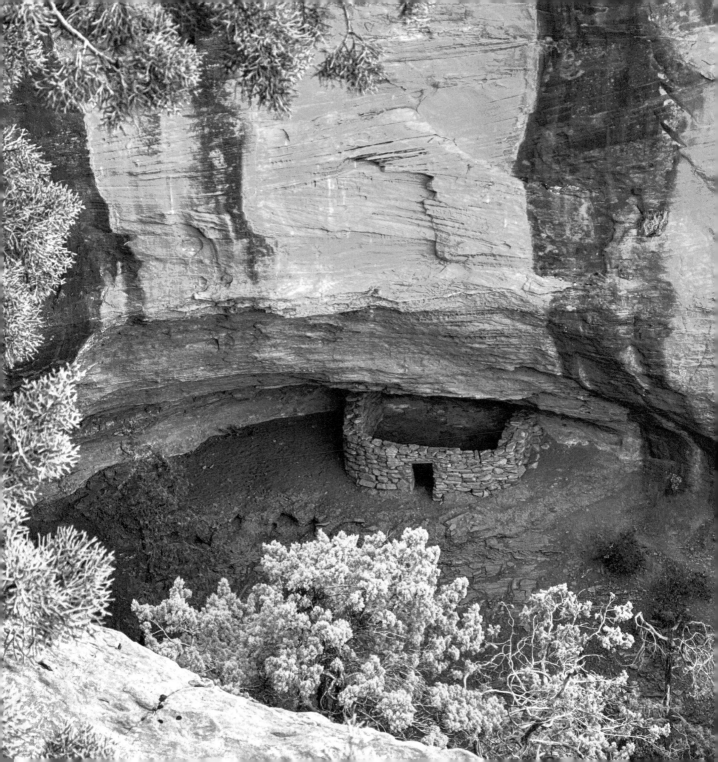

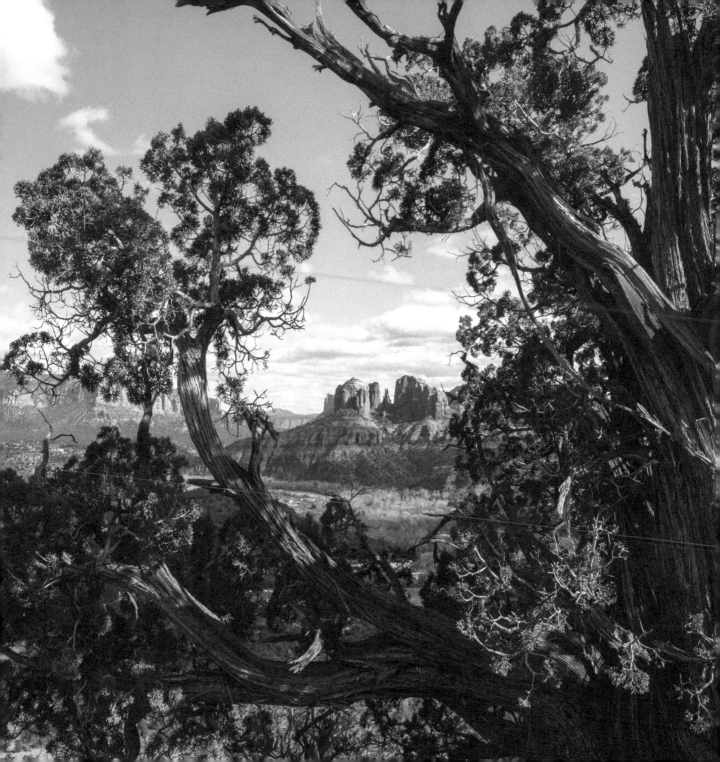

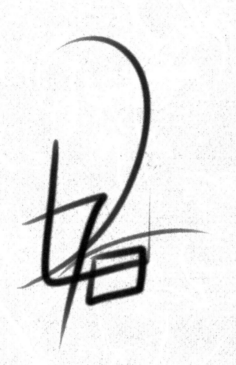

Render

Inside out,
Soul rendering,
Layered brush strokes,
Colored cubes,
Story tellers.

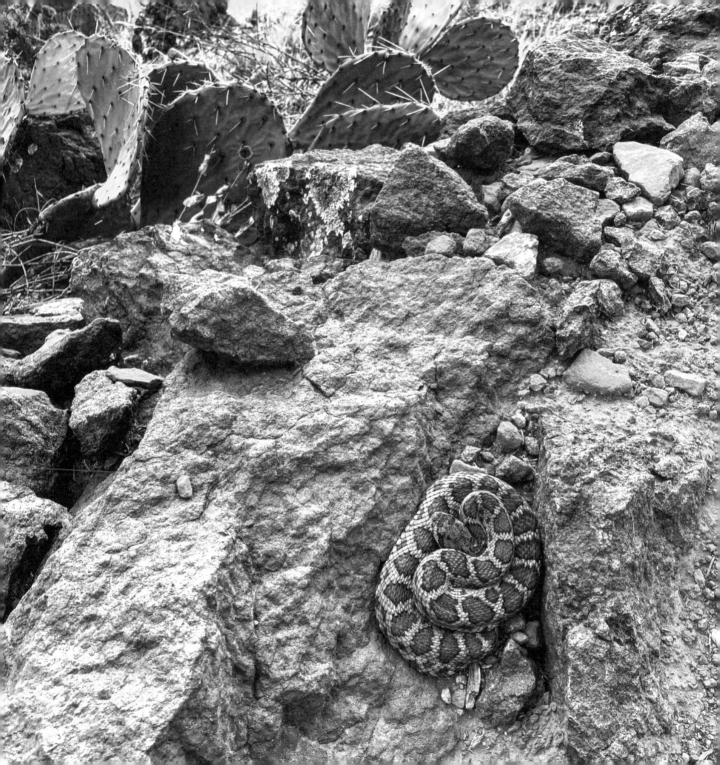

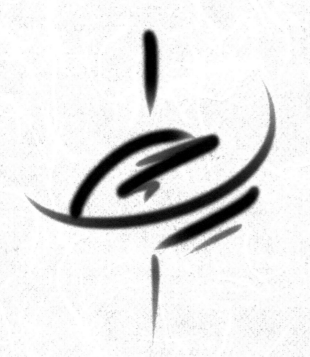

Glimpse

Eyes burn,
Too many
Untold stories
Seen.

27

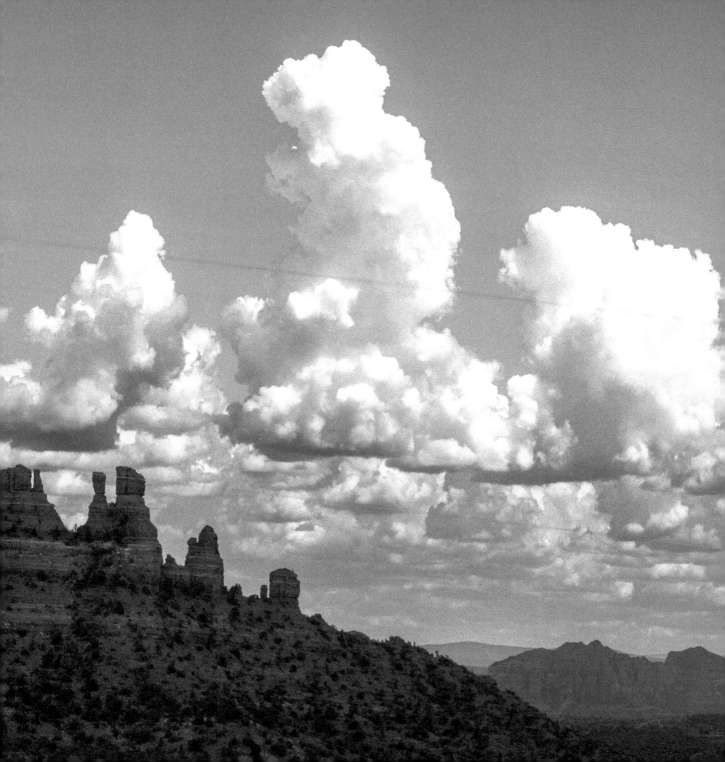

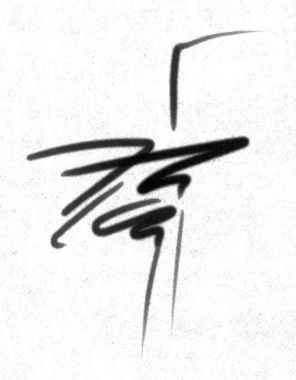

Patience

Wind wipes
Recollections,
Weathered memories,
Through time worn
Rock crevices,
Clarity comes,
In due time.

29

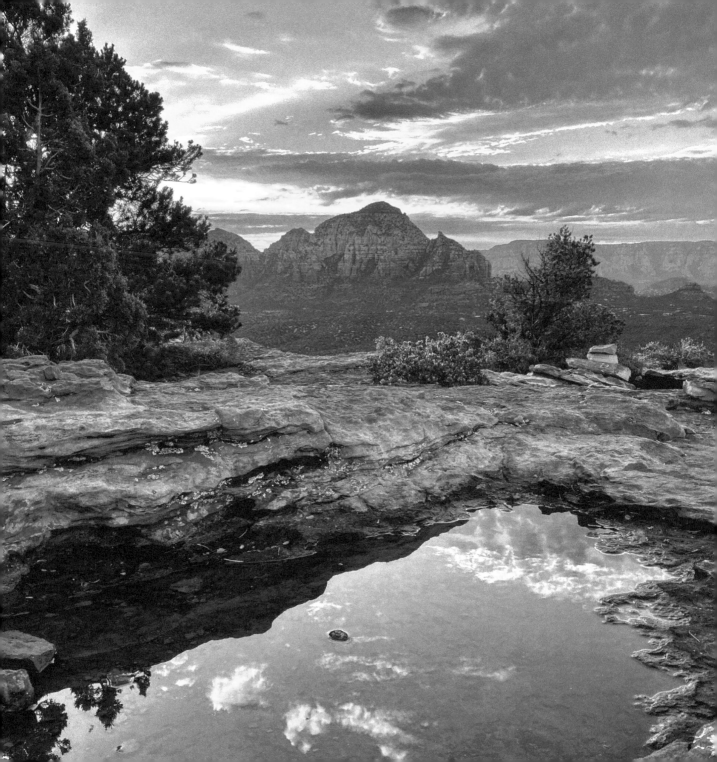

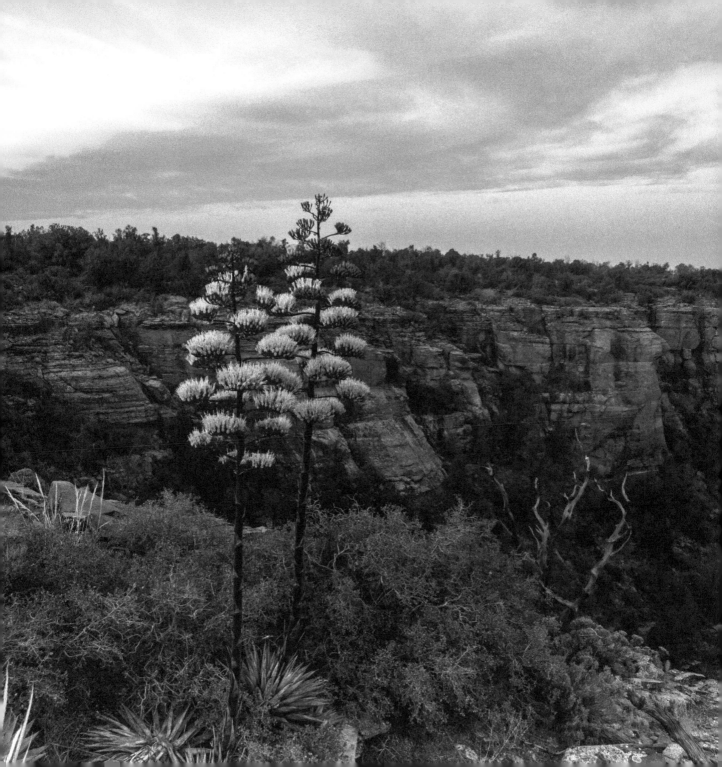

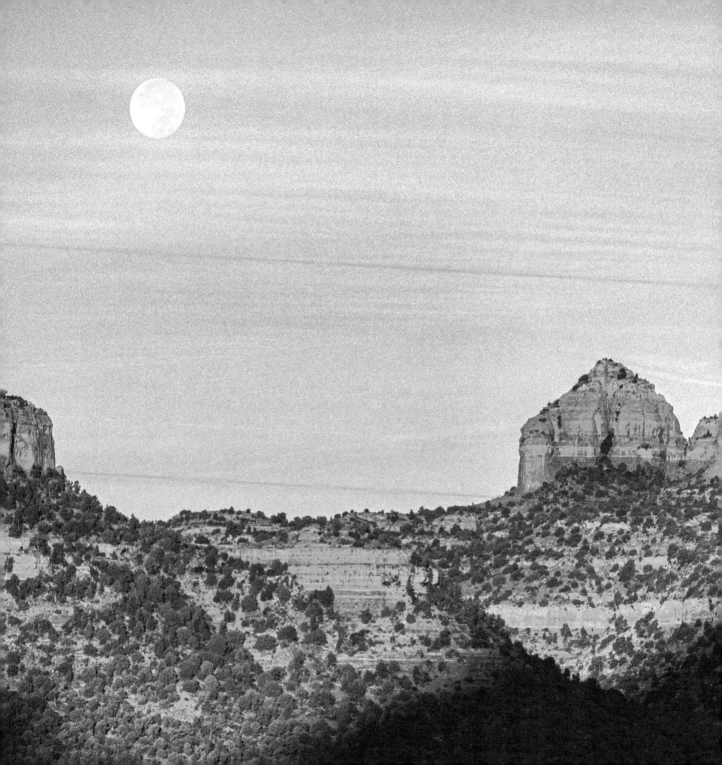

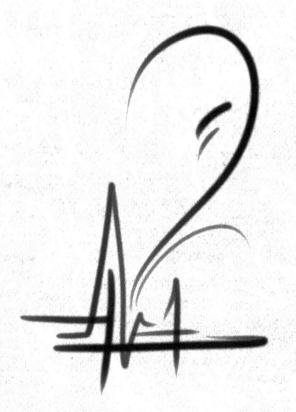

Vast Silence

Echoes off,
Red rock spheres,
Thunder Mountain,
Soul's laughter, tears,
Bounce into space,
Other world,
Letting you in.

33

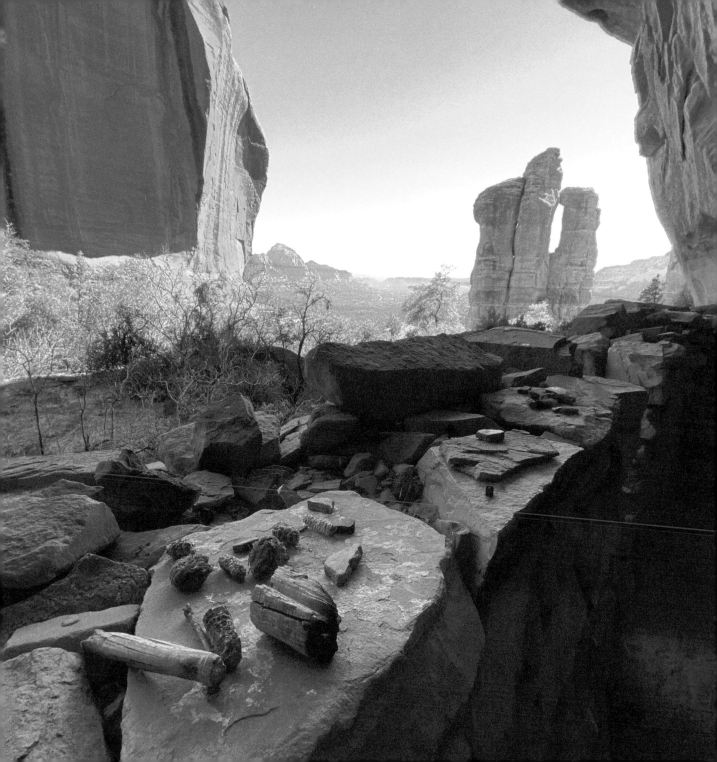

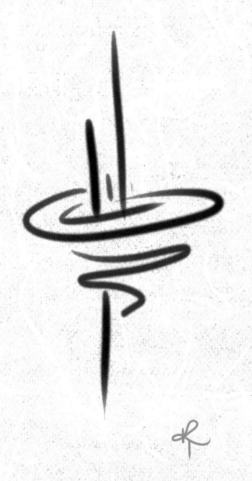

Deep

Carefully cultivated
Interior viewscape,
The better to see
Other's through.

35

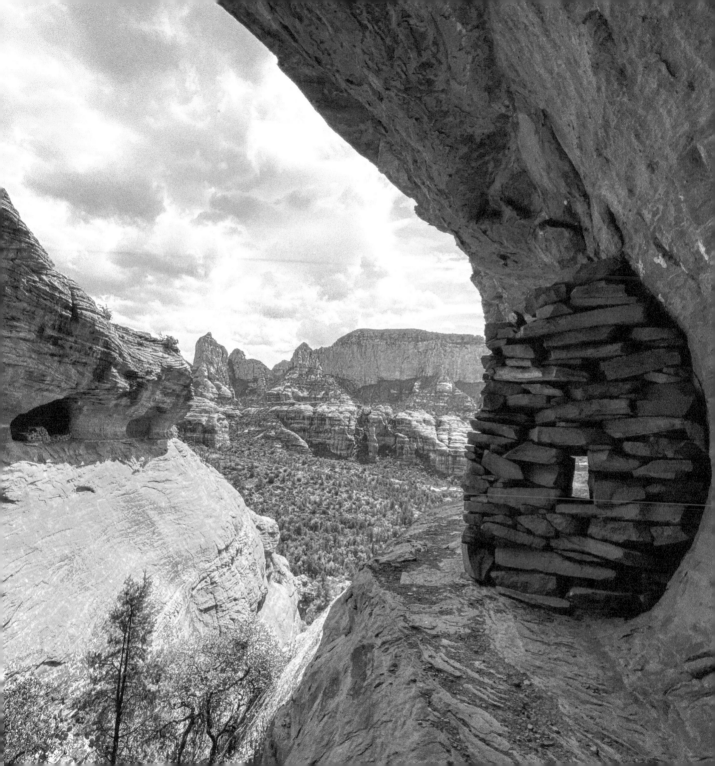

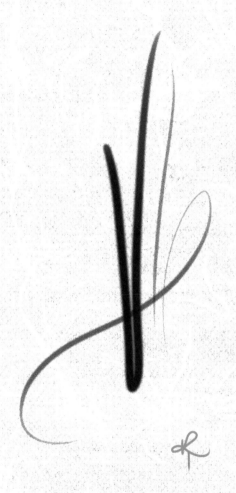

Aging

Removing
Conditioning's
Cloak,
Child like.

37

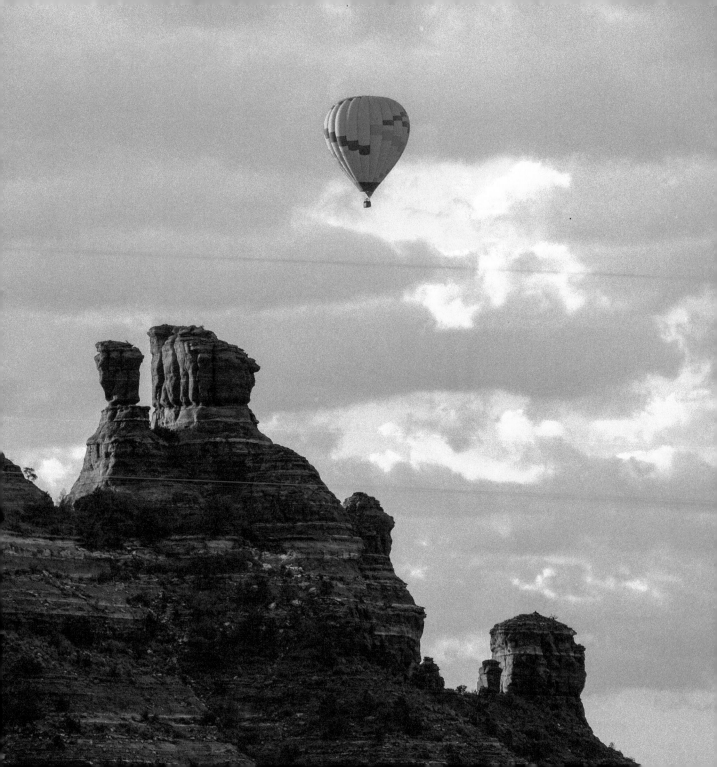

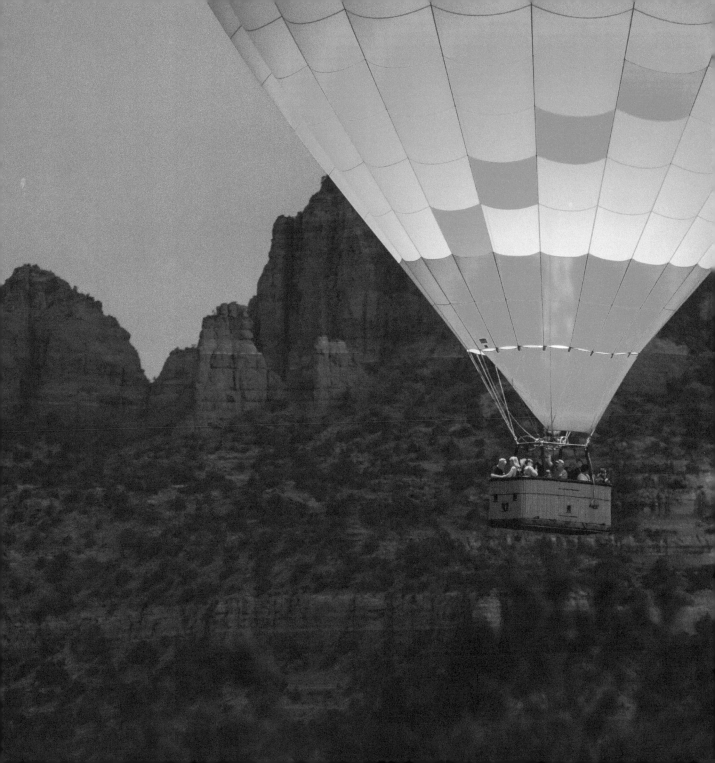

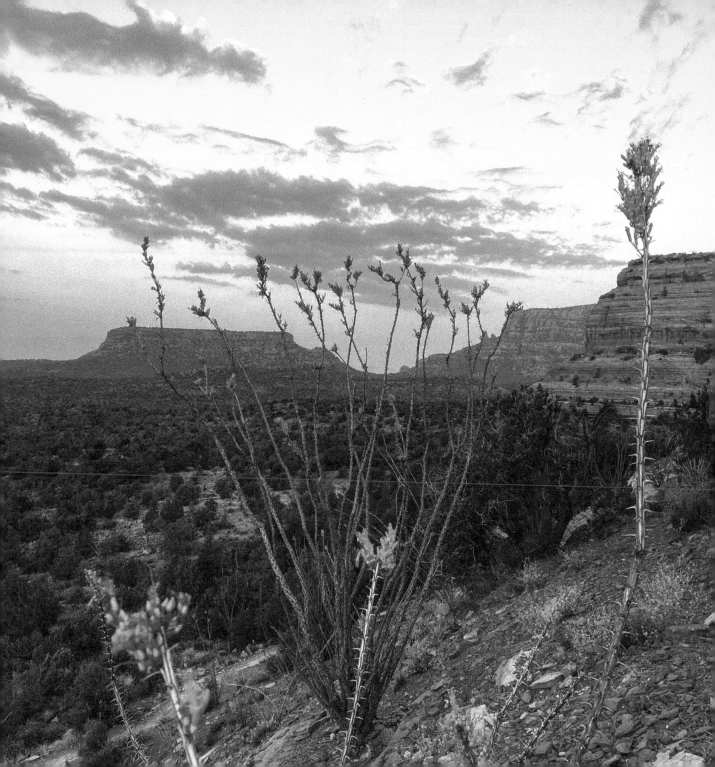

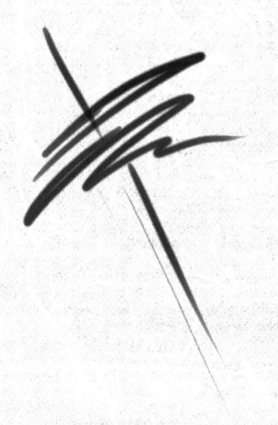

Restive

Weary late
Afternoon sunbeam
Leaks through
Carack in
Dark cloud,
Ready to
Retire.

41

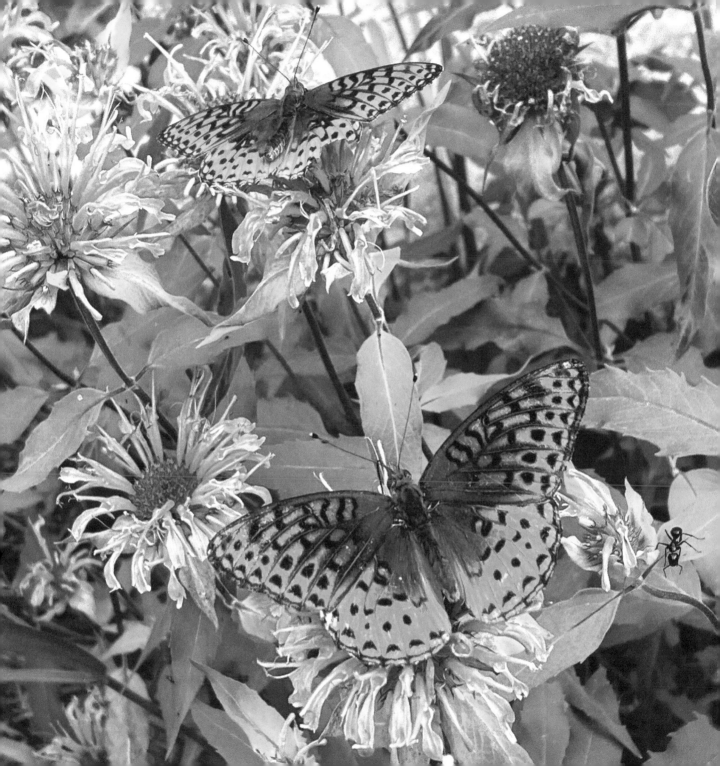

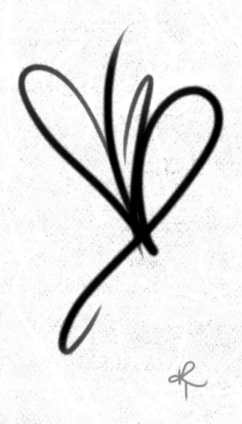

Butterfly

Past's lessons
Echo inside cocoon,
Be still,
Listen, inside,
Ask, Grandmother.

43

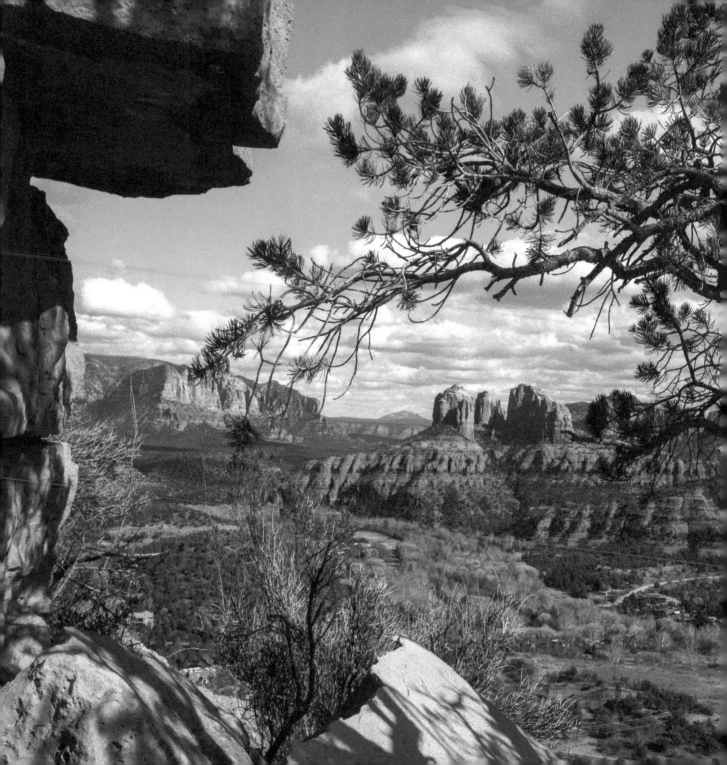

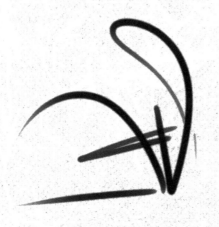

Outlook

Protected ridge
Projected view
Into outback,
Life.

45

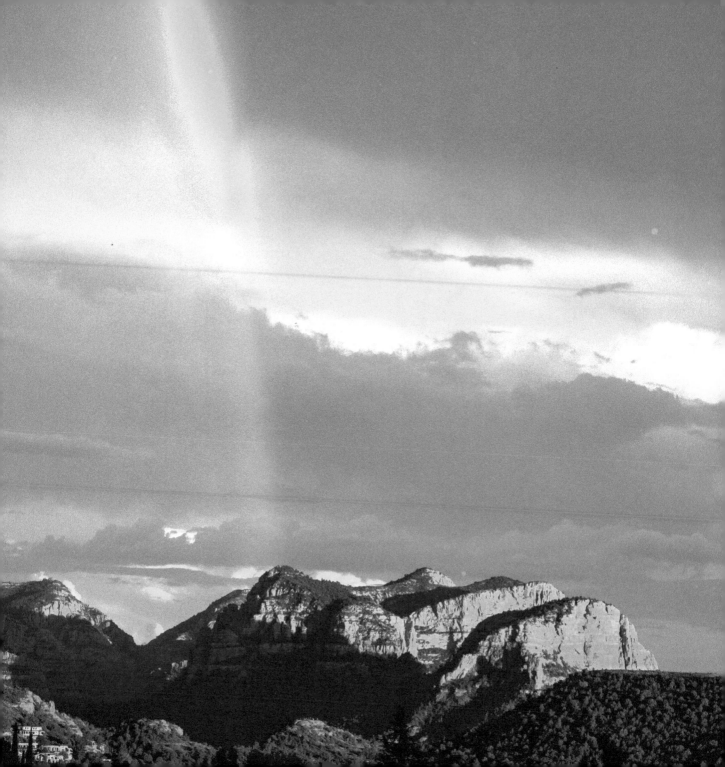

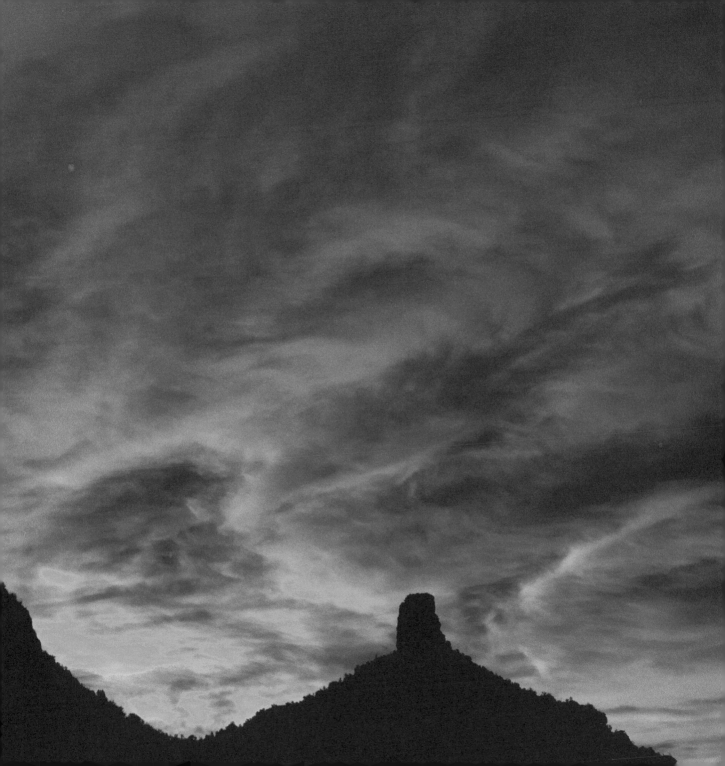

CPSIA information can be obtained
at www.ICGtesting.com
Printed in the USA
BVHW010925231222
654917BV00007B/393